Garf

On Top
Of The World

JIM DAVIS

RAVETTE BOOKS

First published by Ravette Books Limited 1989
Reprinted 1990

Printed and bound in Great Britain
for Ravette Books Limited,
3 Glenside Estate, Star Road, Partridge Green,
Horsham, West Sussex RH13 8RA
by Cox & Wyman Ltd, Reading

ISBN 1 85304 104 1

© 1987 United Feature Syndicate, Inc.

© 1987 United Feature Syndicate, Inc.

© 1987 United Feature Syndicate, Inc.

© 1987 United Feature Syndicate, Inc.

© 1987 United Feature Syndicate, Inc.

JIM DAVIS 11-20

JIM DAVIS 11-25

© 1987 United Feature Syndicate, Inc.

© 1987 United Feature Syndicate, inc.

© 1987 United Feature Syndicate, Inc.

© 1987 United Feature Syndicate, Inc.

JIM DAVIS 12-17

© 1987 United Feature Syndicate, Inc.

© 1988 United Feature Syndicate, Inc.

© 1988 United Feature Syndicate, Inc.

© 1988 United Feature Syndicate, Inc.

© 1988 United Feature Syndicate, Inc.

JIM DAVIS 1-30

© 1988 United Feature Syndicate, Inc.

© 1988 United Feature Syndicate, Inc.

© 1988 United Feature Syndicate, Inc.

2-23   JIM DAVIS

© 1988 United Feature Syndicate, Inc.

SQUEAK

2-24   JIM DAVIS

© 1988 United Feature Syndicate, Inc.

© 1988 United Feature Syndicate, Inc.

JIM DAVIS

3-8

© 1988 United Feature Syndicate, Inc.

JIM DAVIS 3-15

OTHER GARFIELD BOOKS IN THIS SERIES

LANDSCAPE SERIES

COLOUR TV SPECIALS

Here Comes Garfield	£2.95
Garfield On The Town	£2.95
Garfield In The Rough	£2.95
Garfield In Disguise	£2.95
Garfield In Paradise	£2.95
Garfield Goes To Hollywood	£2.95
A Garfield Christmas	£2.95
Garfield's Thanksgiving	£2.95

COLOUR TREASURIES

The Second Garfield Treasury	£5.95
The Third Garfield Treasury	£5.95
The Fourth Garfield Treasury	£5.95

Garfield A Weekend Away	£4.95
Garfield Book Of Cat Names	£2.50
Garfield Best Ever	£4.95
Garfield Selection	£5.95
Garfield How To Party	£3.95
Garfield The Easter Bunny?	£3.95
Garfield His 9 Lives	£5.95

All these books are available at your local bookshop or newsagent, or can be ordered direct from the publisher. Just tick the titles you require and fill in the form below. Prices and availability subject to change without notice.

Ravette Books Limited, 3 Glenside Estate, Star Road, Partridge Green, Horsham, West Sussex RH13 8RA

Please send a cheque or postal order and allow the following for postage and packing. UK: Pocket-books – 45p for one book, 20p for a second book and 15p for each additional book. Landscape Series – 50p for one book plus 30p for each additional book. TV Specials and Cat Names – 45p for one book plus 30p for each additional book. Other titles – 85p for one book plus 50p for each additional book ordered.

Name ....

Address ....

....